Extreme Sports

Written by Adrian Bradbury

Contents

Collins

What are extreme sports?

Extreme sports involve all the action, adventure, thrills and heartaches of other sports, but with added risks. Extreme sportsmen and sportswomen push themselves to the limit. If they go fast, they want to go faster. If they climb high, they want to climb higher. If they find something easy, they want to make it more difficult. They want to challenge themselves, even if it means facing much greater dangers than in ordinary sports.

Most extreme sports are physically tough, so their sportsmen and sportswomen tend to be younger rather than older, but fitness, skill, balance and, above all, training and experience are more important than age.

Fly like a bird

All airborne extreme sports are at the mercy of the weather, which can change quickly and dramatically. Anyone taking part in these sports must decide if they have the skill and experience to cope with the conditions. *Is it safe to jump or fly?*

skydiving

Parachutes were first used as a way of escaping safely from a hot air balloon. Their design and safety improved during the 20th century and jumpers began to use parachutes for sport.

In a typical skydive, the jumpers will leap from a plane at an **altitude** of 3,962 metres. They'll open their parachutes 610 metres above the ground after a **freefall** of one minute.

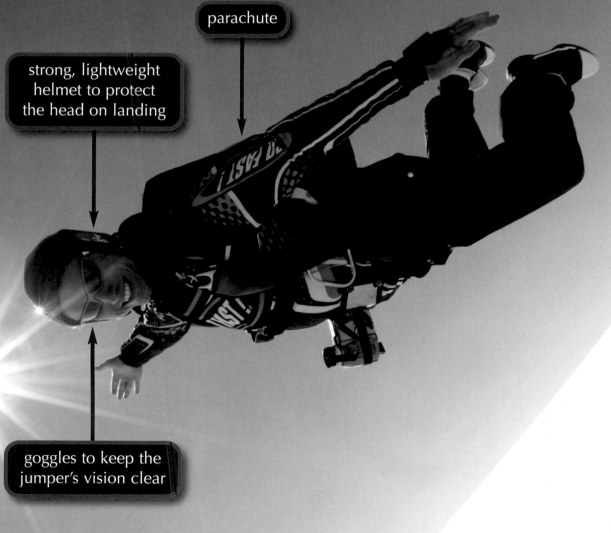

parachute

strong, lightweight helmet to protect the head on landing

goggles to keep the jumper's vision clear

Training and safety

All skydivers take intensive training courses that teach them how to open their **canopy**, how to change their body position in the air and how to land safely.

Sometimes skydivers jump together. This is called formation skydiving.

Extreme skydivers jump higher! Jumps have been made from a height of over 9,144 metres. For these, the skydiver needs to carry bottled oxygen as the air is very thin at that altitude.

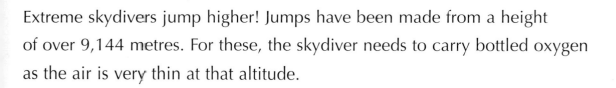

Record breaker

The highest skydive was from an altitude of 31,333 metres by US Captain Joseph Kittinger in 1960. His speed was recorded as 988 kilometres per hour – almost breaking the **sound barrier**.

Wingsuit flying

In order to be able to stay in the air longer, a special suit was designed to slow the jumper down. The wingsuit catches the air, increasing **wind resistance**, or drag, so that the jumper falls at around 97 kilometres per hour when skydiving, rather than the normal speed of 193 kilometres per hour.

The wingsuit is based on the webbed arms and legs of a flying squirrel. For this reason it's often known as a "squirrel suit".

Training and safety

This sport's so difficult to get right that jumpers should have experienced at least 200 skydives before attempting their first wingsuit flight.

The chief developer of the wingsuit, Frenchman Patrick de Gayardon, was killed in 1992 when he jumped to test his latest design.

This wingsuit jumper has a camera attached to his helmet to record his flight.

wings made of of thick nylon

BASE jumping

BASE jumping is one of the most extreme sports invented. Only the most skilful, highly experienced skydivers will ever attempt a BASE jump. All responsible BASE jumpers ask permission first.

Building: usually a city skyscraper

Antenna: a radio tower or mast

To achieve a BASE number, a skydiver must complete jumps from four different starting points. BASE number 1 was given to the first person who managed all four jumps successfully. If you were the 100th person to complete all four jumps, you'd be BASE number 100.

Span: a bridge

Earth: usually off the edge of a cliff

As BASE jumps take place from much lower heights than skydives from planes, the jumpers have less time to open their parachutes, increasing the risk of an accident.

Fortunately, modern rectangular parachutes are designed to open so quickly that they can be used to jump from heights as low as 50 metres. A BASE jumper may even wear a wingsuit so as to have more time to land safely.

On 8 January 2010, Nasr al Niyadi and Omar al Hegelan jumped from a cage suspended from the 160th floor of the newly opened Burj Khalifa skyscraper in Dubai. At 672 metres it was the highest ever BASE jump from a building.

13

Climbing higher

The extreme sport of climbing can be broken down into three main types: rock climbing, ice climbing and mountaineering.

Rock climbing

Climbing up a vertical rock face is a risky sport. A rock climber needs training to master the use of all the different items of equipment.

Good, skilful teamwork lowers the risk of serious injury. It also means that injured climbers have people on hand to help, maybe to save their lives. As well as a first-aid kit, climbers will also carry a mobile phone or two-way radio.

Beginner climbers will start their training on an indoor climbing wall.

Special, thin climbing shoes help climbers to find a foothold and grip the rock. Climbers will also carry a small bag of chalk to help their fingers cling to the rock without slipping.

Climbers are securely clipped to a top rope, so that if they slip they will only fall a short distance.

Helmets are worn to protect a climber's head.

Ice climbing

A more extreme form of rock climbing is ice climbing. This involves climbing up sheer cliff faces covered in ice, or frozen waterfalls.

Unlike rock faces, ice faces appear and disappear as the ice freezes and melts. The climber can experience the thrill of reaching a summit that may soon disappear forever.

An **ice axe** is needed to make **handholds**, as gloved hands cannot grip the slippery ice. On more difficult climbs two axes are needed, one in each hand. Ice screws are used to keep ropes in place.

goggles to protect the eyes from sharp pieces of falling ice

underneath the helmet is a woolly hat for warmth

comfortable, warm clothing to protect against the cold

Ice climbers need to wear **crampons** attached to their boots. These spikes can be driven into the ice to get a firm foothold.

This climber was caught in a small avalanche.

Training and safety

Ice constantly changes and a sudden increase in temperature can make it start to melt. Climbers need to be aware that conditions can change and they must descend as soon as they realise that carrying on would be too dangerous.

Ice climbers carry an avalanche beacon in case of emergency and a shovel to dig themselves out if they become trapped under snow.

They should always allow plenty of time for a climb. Having to descend in darkness is extremely dangerous.

Record breaker

In 2009, Russian Pavel Gulyaev broke the world record for Speed Ice Climbing when he reached the top of a vertical 15-metre ice wall in just 8.75 seconds.

Mountaineering

Mountaineering may include some ice climbing, but it also involves much greater altitudes and distances. There may be a much larger group of climbers, needing extra equipment and possibly a whole support team.

The group will set up a base camp on the mountain where support and supplies can be stored. From there, a small group of climbers will head upwards in an attempt to reach the summit.

base camp

At 8,848 metres, Mount Everest is the highest mountain in the world. It was first conquered in 1953 by Edmund Hillary and Tenzing Norgay.

A group of climbers head towards the summit of Mount Everest

21

Food needs to be carried, as well as cooking equipment, tents, sleeping bags, medical supplies, radios and layers of warm clothing.

Special gloves need to be worn to protect against **frostbite**.

The sun's effects are much greater at the top of a mountain, so climbers always wear sunscreen. Mirrored goggles must be worn to avoid **snow blindness**.

It's unsafe to climb in the dark, so climbers may need to sleep for one or more nights on the mountain, either on a ledge or in a **snow hole**.

Training and safety

Reaching the summit of a mountain may take days or weeks of walking and climbing. Climbers train for months by running, cycling, hiking and weight training.

Altitude sickness, brought on by the thin air, can make climbers feel sick and dizzy. To avoid this, climbers may live at high altitude for a while before climbing, so that their bodies can gradually get used to the difficult breathing conditions.

Further, faster on water

Kitesurfing

Windsurfing was invented when surfing and sailing were combined.

Once sails had been added to surfboards, the next step for an extreme sport was to replace the sail with a kite. The sport of kitesurfing was born. Kitesurfers are called "pilots" rather than "surfers".

helmet →

wetsuit →

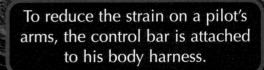

To reduce the strain on a pilot's arms, the control bar is attached to his body harness.

The kite is attached to a control bar by three, four or five lines.

If pilots lose control, they can pull a cord that collapses the kite. The kite can also be released altogether.

Footstraps mean that pilots can stay upright even in high winds.

The most skilful kitesurfers can take off
into the air and keep control of the kite.
Once airborne, they can perform stunts such
as letting go of the control bar with one hand
and grabbing the board, just as a skateboarder
might do. This airborne kind of kitesurfing
makes it more extreme than windsurfing –
crashing down into a wave at high speed
can easily result in serious injury.

Training and safety

Kitesurfers always check the direction and strength of the wind before surfing. Winds blowing in the wrong direction can sweep them out to sea or on to rocks.

They may crash in deep water, so kitesurfers carry a whistle, a two-way radio or a phone.

Kitesurfers should never surf alone. If possible, they should have a partner in a boat who can rescue them quickly if necessary.

Record breaker

In November 2009, Frenchman Alex Caizergues broke his own kitesurfing world record when he reached a speed of 94.4 kilometres per hour.

Further, faster on snow

It's thought that people first used skis to travel on snow over 5,000 years ago. The extreme sport of ski jumping first became popular amongst soldiers in Norway in the early 1800s.

Ski flying

A ski jumper aims to launch himself into the air and land safely over 100 metres further down the side of a mountain, with only a helmet for protection.

Ski flying is a more extreme version of ski jumping. In most ski-jumping competitions, the furthest jump may be 130 to 140 metres. However, a few ski resorts have longer, steeper hills for ski flying, where jumpers can stay in the air longer and cover much greater distances.

In-run: The jumper pushes off from a wooden seat at the start gate, quickly picking up speed as he skis down the steep slope.

Take-off: Having reached a speed of around 96 kilometres an hour, he launches himself into the air off the end of the take-off ramp.

Flight: Once airborne, he pushes his arms out to the sides and tries to make a V-shape with his skis. The V-shape helps to provide maximum lift, allowing the jumper to stay in the air as long as possible.

Landing: Jumpers get marks for style as well as distance, so a correct landing is vital. They should bring their skis back together and land with one foot in front of the other.

29

Training and safety

A beginner will start by taking off from a ramp only a few centimetres high and flying around 10 metres.

Professional ski flyers train for several years as ski jumpers before taking part in ski-flying competitions. Their training includes many hours of gym work.

Wind tunnels are used to perfect a jumper's flying position. Instruments measure how wind resistance increases or decreases as they change their body position.

A ski flyer takes a tumble.

Professional ski-jumping and ski-flying competitions even continue during the summer months. The jumpers land on long sheets of plastic spread across the grass slopes.

Record breaker

The latest ski-flying world record was set in Planica, Slovenia, in 2005, where Norwegian Bjørn Einar Romøren flew 239 metres.

Snowboarding

A snowboard is similar to a skateboard, but without wheels. Its great advantage over skis is that while narrower skis tend to sink into deep, soft snow, the much wider snowboard can glide across the surface. This means that snowboarders can find their way down slopes that would be out of bounds to skiers.

Snowboarding became an Olympic sport in 1998.

helmet

wrist guards

knee pads

Snowboarding is a high-speed sport and may take the boarder on steep slopes through trees or rocks. It's very dangerous, so protective clothing is essential. Sensible snowboarders wear wrist guards and knee pads.

Specially built snow parks allow boarders
to try out stunts such as the 1080° Switch.
The boarder skis backwards down
a take-off ramp and completes three
full turns in the air before landing.

Training and safety

Most snowboarders are already experienced skiers, so they have a good understanding of the dangers of snow sports. As many snowboarders prefer to go **off-piste**, there's a much greater risk of being caught in an avalanche.

Today's snowboarders may wear the latest avalanche life jacket, which inflates automatically. It stops snowboarders from being too deeply buried by the snow if an avalanche occurs, and also helps to keep their heads upright.

A snowboarder going off-piste during an avalanche.

Further, faster on two feet
Ultramarathon

At over 42 kilometres, the marathon is the longest athletics event at the Olympic Games, but some runners like to test themselves over much greater distances. Ultramarathon racing was invented for them.

The Marathon des Sables (Marathon of the Sands) is one of the toughest running events in the world. Runners cover a distance of 243 kilometres in six separate races over six days in the intense heat of the Sahara Desert.

Record breaker

Moroccan running legend Lahcen Ahansal won the Marathon des Sables every year between 1999 and 2007. His brother, Mohamad, won it in 2008, 2009 and 2010.

Training and safety

Long-distance runners train for many months before a big race, gradually increasing the distance they run.

One of the main dangers for runners is knowing when to stop. They must listen to the messages their muscles and heart are sending out and stop when their health is at risk.

These runners are wearing special covers to stop sand from getting into their running shoes.

Adventure racing

Adventure racing is the most extreme sport of all – one that tests skill, bravery, speed, strength, endurance and willpower. Challenges may involve rock climbing, **caving**, mountain biking, horse riding, swimming, mountaineering, **white-water kayaking** and even **scuba diving**.

In the longer events, teams set off on a six-day course with only a map and compass to guide them to their final destination. Courses can cover distances as great as 800 kilometres, through deserts, mountains, forests or over ice.

Training and safety

Before taking on such a challenging race, runners need to train together to become a tight-knit team. They all need to be very fit and their team should contain a mix of experts in all the different sports that make up the race.

All entrants must pass a series of tests before the start of the race to prove that they have the necessary skills and fitness to complete the course.

Record breaker

In 2010, Rajesh Durbal completed the Resolution Adventure Race in Canada, despite competing with two false legs. Rajesh's limbs had been amputated before he was one year old.

We are the champions!

The Olympic Games

Some extreme sports don't have regular competitions, but a few are part of the greatest sporting show on Earth, the Olympic Games.

Swiss ski jumper, Simon Ammann, receiving a Gold medal at the 2010 Winter Olympics.

American snowboarder Seth Wescott wins Gold at the 2010 Winter Olympics.

World Championships

For other extreme sportsmen and sportswomen there's World Championship glory to aim for.

For all of these champions the medals are a fitting reward for all the hours, weeks, months and even years of painful, exhausting and dangerous training they have gone through.

The British women's bobsleigh team winning Gold at the World Championships in America, 2009, where extreme speeds of over 147 kilometres an hour were reached.

Glossary

altitude	the height above sea level
canopy	the fabric part of a parachute, not including the lines
caving	the sport of exploring caves, often deep underground
crampons	metal plates with spikes fixed to boots to help with rock climbing or walking on ice
freefall	the period of fall before a parachute is opened
frostbite	severe injuries to the body, caused by extreme cold
handholds	lumps or cracks in the rock where fingers can get a firm grip
ice axe	special axe for cutting into ice, with one pointed end and one flattened end and a spike at the foot
off-piste	away from the prepared ski runs on a mountain
professional	someone who's paid to play a sport, or receives prize money
scuba diving	diving below the surface of the sea, wearing oxygen tanks and breathing tubes
snow blindness	temporary blindness caused by light reflected from a large area of snow
snow hole	a hole cut into snow that is used for temporary shelter
sound barrier	the speed of sound (around 343 metres per second)
white-water kayaking	paddling a small boat down a rocky, fast-flowing river
wind resistance	the force of air pushing against something
wind tunnels	small rooms where a strong jet of air can be blown against a person or aircraft, to copy the conditions when they fly at high speed

Index

Taking it to extremes!

Jumping higher

Climbing higher

46

Travelling faster on land and sea

Against the odds

Running longer

World glory

 Ideas for guided reading

Learning objectives: deduce characters' reasons for behaviour from their actions and explain how ideas are developed in non-fiction texts; use knowledge of different organisational features of text to find information; identify and summarise evidence from a text to support a hypothesis; create roles showing how behaviour can be interpreted from different viewpoints

Curriculum links: PE: Outdoor and adventurous activities

Interest words: altitude, canopy, caving, crampons, freefall, frostbite, handholds, ice axe, off-piste, professional, scuba diving, snow blindness, snow hole, sound barrier, white-water kayaking, wind resistance, wind tunnel, kitesurfing, wingsuit flying, ultramarathon, ski flying, ski jumping

Resources: writing materials, ICT

Getting started

This book may be read over two or more guided reading sessions.

- Look at the photograph on the cover together. Ask the children some questions to stimulate discussion, e.g. *What sport is taking place? Where could the photograph have been taken?*

- Ask one of the children to read the blurb aloud. Discuss what "extreme sports" the children know about. *What makes a sport "extreme"?* e.g. weather, height, water, location.

- Discuss sports the children enjoy and whether any of the sports are dangerous or "extreme".

Reading and responding

- Ask a child to read pp2–3 aloud and discuss the illustrations. Ask children what qualities you need for extreme sports and why people like to engage in them.

- Working in pairs, ask children to use the contents page to choose a section to read, making sure all the chapters are covered. Ask them to make notes in order to help them describe a particular sport. Suggest that they summarise using bullet points rather than copy the information.

- Remind children to use the glossary to explain unfamiliar words.